Will You Sign My Petition?

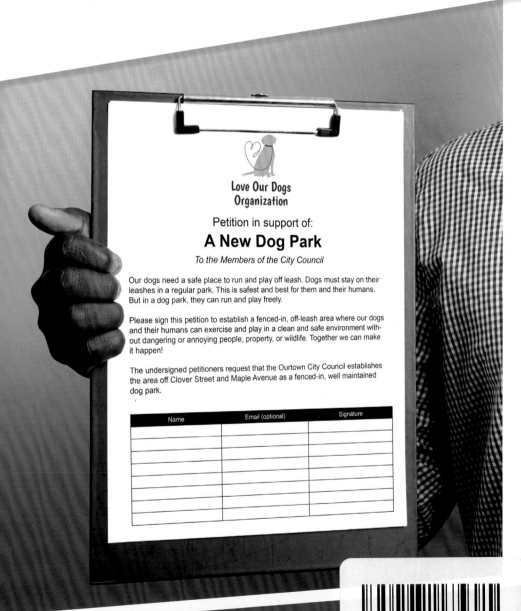

Love Our Dogs Organization

Petition in support of:

A New Dog Park

To the Members of the City Council

Our dogs need a safe place to run and play off leash. Dogs must stay on their leashes in a regular park. This is safest and best for them and their humans. But in a dog park, they can run and play freely.

Please sign this petition to establish a fenced-in, off-leash area where our dogs and their humans can exercise and play in a clean and safe environment without dangering or annoying people, property, or wildlife. Together we can make it happen!

The undersigned petitioners request that the Ourtown City Council establishes the area off Clover Street and Maple Avenue as a fenced-in, well maintained dog park.

Name	Email (optional)	Signature

Stephanie Kraus

Reader Consultants

Cheryl Norman Lane, M.A.Ed.
Classroom Teacher
Chino Valley Unified School District

Jennifer M. Lopez, M.S.Ed., NBCT
Teacher Specialist—History/Social Studies
Norfolk Public Schools

iCivics Consultants

Emma Humphries, Ph.D.
Chief Education Officer

Taylor Davis, M.T.
Director of Curriculum and Content

Natacha Scott, MAT
Director of Educator Engagement

Publishing Credits

Rachelle Cracchiolo, M.S.Ed., *Publisher*
Emily R. Smith, M.A.Ed., *VP of Content Development*
Véronique Bos, *Creative Director*
Dona Herweck Rice, *Senior Content Manager*
Dani Neiley, *Associate Content Specialist*
Fabiola Sepulveda, *Series Designer*

Image Credits: p.11 David Becker/Getty Images; pp.12–13 Don Gray Universal Images Group/Newscom; p.14 Library of Congress [LC-USZ62-30776]; p.16 Leonard Ortiz/Zuma Press/Newscom; p.18 Bryan Smith/Zuma Press/Newscom; p.19 Frances M. Roberts/ Newscom; pp.20–21 Dan Cappellazzo/AP Images for Crayola; p.25 Jemal Countess/Getty Images for Parents Together; p. 28 Getty Images/Drew Angerer/ p.29 Danita Delimont Photography/Newscom; all other images from iStock and/or Shutterstock

Library of Congress Cataloging-in-Publication Data

Names: Kraus, Stephanie, author.
Title: Will you sign my petition? / Stephanie Kraus.
Description: Huntington Beach, CA : Teacher Created Materials, 2020. |
  Series: iCivics | Includes index. | Audience: Grades 2-3 | Summary: "The
  United States of America is known as the 'land of the free.' American
  citizens can share their thoughts and ideas freely. That includes to
  right to petition. Every day, people petition for change in their
  communities. They hope the changes will make the world a better place to
  live"-- Provided by publisher.
Identifiers: LCCN 2020016211 (print) | LCCN 2020016212 (ebook) | ISBN
  9781087605081 (paperback) | ISBN 9781087619279 (ebook)
Subjects: LCSH: Petition, Right of--United States--Juvenile literature. |
  Petitions--United States--Juvenile literature. | Political
  participation--United States--Juvenile literature.
Classification: LCC KF4780 .K73 2020 (print) | LCC KF4780 (ebook) | DDC
  323.4/80973--dc23
LC record available at https://lccn.loc.gov/2020016211
LC ebook record available at https://lccn.loc.gov/2020016212

5482 Argosy Avenue
Huntington Beach, CA 92649-1039
www.tcmpub.com

ISBN 978-1-0876-0508-1

Table of Contents

Following the Rules

Rules are all around us. Your school might have a rule about how long you can play at recess. Your parents might have a rule about your bedtime. Your grandparents might make you eat all your dinner before you have dessert. You might agree with the rules. Or you might **disagree** with them.

A son asks to hear a story before bedtime.

If you have ever wanted to change a rule, you are not alone. People around the world are working to change rules and **laws** all the time. Sometimes, people feel that rules are unfair. Other times, they think new rules are needed.

It is common to want to change a rule, but it can also be hard to get your voice heard. To help change rules or laws, many people use **petitions**.

No dogs
Penalties apply

Jump into Fiction

Helping Hands

Brian is so excited for his family vacation. It will be his first time on a beach!

Brian and his dad walk from the hotel to the beach. They jump in the cool water and start swimming. They see beautiful fish all around them. They even see a huge sea turtle!

Brian swims close to the turtle to get a better look. He spies something around its neck. It is a plastic bag! He looks around and sees other garbage in the water too.

His dad says that plastic in the water is a big problem. Animals get trapped in it, or they try to eat it and get sick. Brian loves animals and does not want to see them hurt.

On the walk back from the beach, Brian is worried. He thinks about all the plastic he uses. Then, Brian thinks about the grocery store where he lives. The store uses hundreds of plastic bags every day. This gives Brian an idea.

Brian writes a petition to the grocery store owners. He asks them to stop using plastic bags in the store. Brian writes that a lot of bags end up in the ocean. He tells about the turtle he saw. Brian suggests that customers bring their own bags to the store.

At school, Brian asks his teachers and friends to sign his petition. He talks to people in town too. They like Brian's idea. Brian gets over two hundred people to sign!

Brian takes his petition to the store. To his surprise, the store owners agree with him! They say they will stop using plastic bags.

Ban Plastic Bags!

Every year, hundreds of plastic bags end up in landfills or the oceans. The plastic used in bags can take 1,000 years to decompose! These bags are wasteful and very harmful to the environment. We can easily replace them with faster decomposing paper bags and reusable green bags.

The undersigned petitioners request that this grocery store stops using single-use plastic bags.

Name	Email (optional)	Signature

Back to Nonfiction

Being a Good Citizen

Brian made a change in his town. He was being a good **citizen**. A good citizen cares about their community.

Being a citizen means you have rights. These rights are part of a **democracy**. U.S. citizens and residents have the right to speak their minds. They have the right to create petitions. Citizens who are 18 or older have the right to vote for their leaders too.

People under 18 cannot vote for elected leaders. But that doesn't mean they shouldn't pay attention to elections. They can learn about issues. They can make up their own minds. They can be **informed** about the issues that matter most to them. They can ask leaders to make changes. One way to do that is to create petitions.

These good citizens clean their beaches.

Being a Good Voter

People running for **office** talk about things they want to change. Good voters listen and think. They decide whether they agree or disagree with what is being said. Then, they choose leaders based on those decisions.

What Is a Petition?

A petition is a letter that explains a problem. Petitions are sent to people who are in charge or who make decisions. They can be used to make things better.

Petition writers want to get a lot of people to sign their petitions. When people sign their names, it means they agree with the ideas.

Petitions can be hard to organize. The person in charge of the petition has a tough job. They need to clearly explain the problem they see. Then, they have to offer a **solution** to the problem. People may not like their idea. Some people may think it will make things worse. Other people may think it is better to keep things as they are. It is the job of the petition writer to **persuade** others.

Spread the Word!

People may try to talk to others about problems they see. This is called *raising awareness*. It is a key part of organizing a petition.

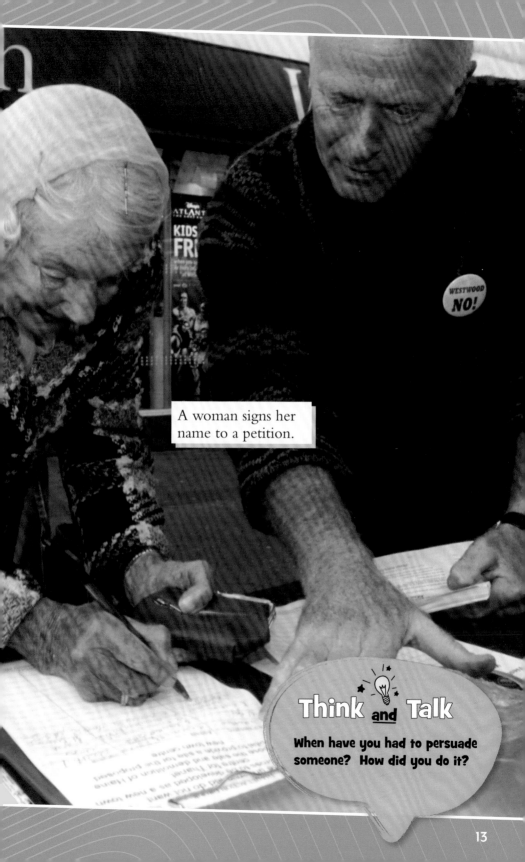

A woman signs her name to a petition.

Think and Talk

When have you had to persuade someone? How did you do it?

Petitions have been used for thousands of years. They have helped a lot of people fight for equal treatment.

In 1866, a group of women created a petition. They wanted to change the law so they would be allowed to vote. Their petition was ignored at first. But the group did not give up. They wrote more petitions and held parades. They wanted people to care. Women finally gained the right to vote in 1920.

Women's vote supporters ask people to sign their petition in 1912.

Petitions are used often today. In some parts of the world, children are not allowed or able to go to school. They have to work. There are petitions to change this practice. People think every child has the right to learn.

Big issues like this often need more than just petitions. But petitions are a good way to spread your message and fight for change.

A Brave Voice

Malala Yousafzai (YOO-suhf-zy) wrote a petition. Where she lived, girls were often not allowed to go to school. She wanted them all to have this right. Her petition got more than one million signatures in just one month.

Many children, like this girl in Nepal, must work instead of go to school.

Petitions Today

Petitions have changed over the years. People used to write them by hand. Then, they would walk around their communities and talk to people. They would explain the issues and share their solutions. They might stand in **town squares** or knock on doors. Years later, people used telephones to spread the word. Either way, it took a very long time to get signatures.

This petition volunteer stands outside a store asking for signatures.

Now, most petitions are online. People can read about issues around the world. They can **digitally** sign their names. They can share petitions with other people too. That helps spread the word. Getting signatures is now much quicker than it was in the past.

This online petition has over 1.5 million signatures.

The First One?

People who study history think they may have found the first petition. It was written by people who were building the pyramids in ancient Egypt. They asked for better working conditions.

Kids and Petitions

A lot of petitions try to help students. For instance, there are petitions to make school food healthier. Those petitions say that school lunches should have more fruits and vegetables. Some parents disagree. They say school food is healthy as it is. They say if students don't like the new options, they might not eat as much as they need.

There are also petitions to start school later. Many parents want school to start after 8 a.m. They say it would help students feel better during the day. It could lead to better grades. Other parents say that it would be too hard for their families. They wouldn't be able to drop off their children at school and still get to work on time.

Both of these types of petitions want to make school better. But it can be hard to find something that works for everyone.

This student asks for more money for after-school programs.

Mike Bloomberg,
I Like afterschool because They let me do my homework We get to go outside when it is hot. we go on fun and exciting trips. Our best are they about we eat healthy Snacks here I enjoy reading and art.

From,
Ashley

Longer Lunches

Some petitions want to make lunchtime longer. Some schools have lunch breaks that are 15 or 20 minutes long. Other schools have 30-minute lunches.

Students sign a giant petition asking for a new school to be built.

Anyone can start a petition. It does not matter how old you are. In fact, a lot of kids start petitions. Sometimes, those are the ones that work the best! One of those petitions came from a class in California. The students thought about all the markers they use in class. They knew old markers went in the trash. The ink made it so that the markers could not be **recycled**. The students wished they could recycle the plastic. So, they wrote a petition. It was **addressed** to Crayola®. They asked for a way to recycle used markers. Tens of thousands of people signed the petition!

Change did not happen right away. But after a year, it worked! Crayola® started a program. People can now mail in old markers. The plastic gets recycled. Many schools now use the program.

A worker recycles used markers.

Recycling Success

In its first five years, the Crayola® program recycled more than 70 tons of plastic markers. That's about the same weight as 10 Tyrannosaurus rexes!

A Holiday Petition

Not all petitions are for serious problems. Some are used for fun things too!

In 2018, a fun petition made the news. It focused on Halloween. The holiday is often on a weeknight. Young people have to go to school the next day. So, it can be hard to stay out late. The petition said Halloween should be moved to Saturday. Young people could trick or treat and not have to wake up early the next day. They would not be tired at school.

Thousands of people signed the petition. But many others did not. A lot of people don't have strong feelings about it. It can be hard to get people to care about issues like these. Petition writers need to think about who would care most. Then, they have to find ways to get their attention.

One Sweet Deal!

A lot of candy companies supported the Halloween petition. They knew people would have to buy more candy if young people could trick or treat for longer. Snickers® even gave out one million free bars to gain support!

Think and Talk

Who would you ask to sign a Halloween petition? Why?

Writing Your Own Petition

There are some questions to ask yourself before starting a petition. What is the problem I want to solve? What is my solution? Who would my petition help? Could it lead to other problems? How can I spread the word?

Once you answer those questions, you can start writing the petition. You should write your petition as a letter. It should be addressed to the person or company with the power to change things. You should tell them why the issue means so much to you. Be sure to use kind words. After all, you are trying to change someone's mind!

One of the most important parts of a petition is spreading the word. You have to tell others why the change would help them too. The more signatures you have, the more seriously your request will be taken.

Review Your Work!

Remember to have an adult read your petition. They can help you catch any mistakes you might have missed! A well-written letter will show that you are serious about making a change.

These students got 1.5 million signatures for their petition.

It can take months or years for a petition to cause real change. Some petitions never do. There could be a lot of reasons why this happens. People may not agree with the new idea. Or maybe not enough people read the petition. It can be hard to raise awareness. But that doesn't mean people shouldn't write petitions! Even if they don't cause things to change, they can still help solve problems.

Petitions with a lot of signatures are often in the news. People might see petitions on television. They might read about them online. People may post about the issues to spread the word. That can help petitions get more signatures.

Petitions can also help raise money. People may choose to donate to the cause. Or they might **volunteer** their time. These actions can help change things even when petitions do not work.

Young people hold a protest for a cause.

Helping the World

Petitions are a way for people to show they care. People care about their community. They care about their friends and family. If something is unfair, they speak up! They get involved.

Before you start a petition, talk to your friends, family, and teachers. Ask them what they think. It is good to talk about problems before trying to solve them. You may learn something you did not know. You may come up with better solutions.

Creating petitions is one of our rights. It is a right guaranteed in the First Amendment. Petitions are also a great way to help others. They prove that people working together can solve problems.

So, think about what issues matter most to you. What changes would you like to see? Then, get writing!

These children protest for better schools.

Warming temperatures harm polar bears.

Think and Talk

How might a petition help the polar bears? Would this picture help the petition?

Glossary

addressed—written to someone or something

citizen—a person who legally belongs to a country and has the rights of that country; a member of a community

democracy—a form of government in which people vote for their leaders

digitally—done using computers or electronic devices

disagree—have a different opinion

informed—aware and knowledgeable

laws—the set of rules made by the government of a place

office—a position or job in government

persuade—to convince someone to do something by asking or giving reasons

petitions—formal requests made to people or organizations to change or do something

recycled—turned into something new

solution—something that solves a problem

town squares—the main public areas in towns

volunteer—work for free

Index

Civics in Action

Part of being a good community member means trying to make things better for your community. You have the power to make a change. It is your turn to try to solve a problem. It can be a problem at your school or in your community. You may want to change a rule or make a new one. Follow these steps to write a petition:

1. Identify a problem or need.

2. Work with others to think of a solution.

3. Write a petition. Explain the problem and how you want to solve it.

4. Make a plan to spread the word and get signatures.

5. Decide on the right person or group to submit your petition to. Then, submit your petition.